Green
Book
2

JUNIOR
READING Start

KB173805

I am books

THE JUNIOR READING Start

Green Book 2

© 2011 I am Books

Published by
I am Books
327-32   1116ho, Daeroung Techno Town 12cha
Gasan-dong, Kumcheon-gu, Seoul, Korea 153-802
TEL 82-2-6343-0999
FAX 82-2-6343-0995~6
www.iambooks.co.kr

Publisher	Sangwook Oh, Sunghyun Shin
Author	TIMES CORE The Junior Times
Editor	Sungwon Lee, Dahhyun Gang, Jinhee Lee
Design	Mijung Oh, Ran Park
Illustrations	Soyoung Cho
Marketing	Shindong Jang, Shinkuk Jo, Misun Jang

ISBN 978-89-6398-068-3 64740

Green
Book
2

JUNIOR
READING Start

How to **Study** This Book

01 Before reading articles, listen to audio files carefully two or three times.

02 Underline words that you are not familiar with, reading aloud the article.

03 Read the article one more time, making a guess the meaning of words.

04 Look up the dictionary to find out the meaning of words.

05 Memorize words that you don't know and try to solve the word tip quiz.

06 Read the article once again and answer the questions.

07 Lastly, listen to the audio file one more time focusing on the words you've learned.

CONTENTS

I Still Enjoy Driving!

Look at the old lady in the picture. Her name is Elza Ronis and she lives in Australia. She is 98 years old, but she can still drive! In fact, she is the oldest driver in Australia! "I started driving in 1949. I still enjoy driving very much. I feel excited when I drive my car." she said. She often drives to visit her family and friends. Drive safely, Mrs. Ronis!

Staff reporter Erica Choi

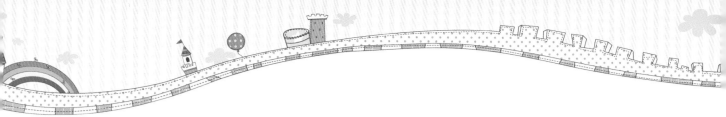

Comprehension I

Read each question and find the right answer.

(a) What is the main topic of the article?

① An old lady who can drive a car

② An old lady who got a driver's license

③ An old lady who makes cars

④ An old lady who can fix cars

(b) Write down three words that begin with 'F' in the article.

① _____

② _____

③ _____

(c) When did she start driving?

She _____ .

Word Tip

▌still	▌in fact	▌the oldest (old의 최상급)	▌driver
_____	_____	_____	_____
▌~하는 것을 즐기다	▌들뜨다, 신나다	▌자주, 종종	▌안전운전 하세요
_____	_____	_____	_____

Vocabulary

Choose the right words to complete each sentence.

(a) She is 98 years old, but she can still drive! _____, she is the oldest driver in Australia!

① In fact

② Therefore

③ So

④ Thus

(b) I still enjoy _____ very much.

① drive

② driving

③ driver

④ to drive

(c) I felt _____ when I started driving my car.

① to exciting

② exciting

③ excited

④ asked

Look at the picture below and then answer the questions.

(a) Who is she?

① She is an old lady who enjoys driving.

② She is an old lady who enjoys listening to music.

③ She is an old lady who enjoys exercising.

④ She is an old lady who enjoys swimming.

(b) Where does she drive to?

① She drives to visit the supermarket.

② She drives to go to the gym.

③ She drives to go to the grocery store.

④ She drives to visit her family and friends.

(c) How old is she?

① She is 100 years old.

② She is 98 years old.

③ She is over 100 years old.

④ She is 89 years old.

Which Country Eats the Most Cheese?

Many people all over the world love eating cheese. The US is the top producer of cheese in the world. Then, which country eats the most cheese? No, it is not the US. The country is in Europe. It's Greece! Each person in Greece eats about 28 kilograms of cheese a year! That's a lot of cheese!

Staff reporter Daniel Chang

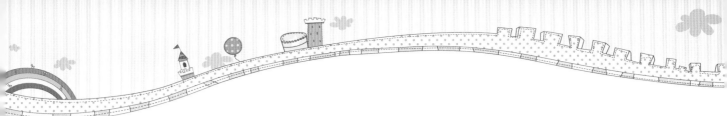

 **Question** 01

Comprehension

Which is NOT true about the article? Read the following sentences and then correct the wrong ones.

(a) The US is the top producer of cheese in the world.

→ _____.

(b) People in the US eat the most cheese in the world.

→ _____.

(c) Many people all over the world love eating cheese.

→ _____.

(d) Each person in Greece eats about 28 kilograms of cheese a month.

→ _____.

Word Tip

▮ all over the world	▮ top	▮ producer	▮ country
_____	_____	_____	_____
▮ Europe	▮ Greece	▮ 각각의	▮ 사람
_____	_____	_____	_____
▮ 많은			
_____			

 **Grammar**

Circle the right words to complete each sentence.

(a) [**Which** / Where / How] country eats the most cheese?

(b) Have you ever [**visited** / visits / visit] Greece?

(c) The country which [eat / is eaten / **eats**] the most cheese is in Europe.

(d) What kinds of cheese do you enjoy [to eat / **eating** / ate] ?

 Question Writing

Look at the picture below. Complete the sentences to answer the questions.

(a) **What is this?** → It is a _____.

(b) **What is it special?** → Because it is _____ by people all over the world.

(c) **Which country eats the most cheese?**

→ People in _____ eat the most cheese in the world.

04 Question Vocabulary

Let's think of some words or phrases that could be used to describe the cheese. Fill in the blanks.

(a) **People started e __ __ __ __ __ cheese more than 4,000 years**

a__ __.

(b) **Cheese is very r __ __ __ in calcium.**

(c) **Cheese is good for your b__ __ __ __.**

(d) **Mozzarella, cream cheese, and cheddar cheese are very**

p __ __ __ __ __ __.

Can Animals Laugh or Cry?

We, humans, often laugh and cry. We laugh when we are happy. We cry when we are sad. But can animals laugh or cry, too? Dogs and other animals can shed tears. But their tears are used to moisten their eyes. They don't cry to express sadness. Animals cannot smile to express happiness, either. Only humans can do that!

Staff reporter Daniel Chang

14

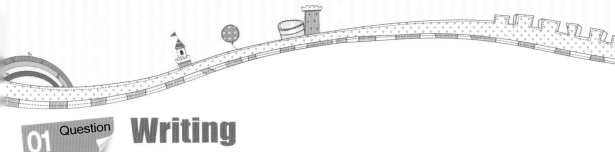

01 Question Writing

Complete the sentences by filling in the blanks.

(a) We, humans, o __ __ __ __ laugh and cry.

(b) We l __ __ __ __ when we are happy.

(c) Can a __ __ __ __ __ __ laugh or cry, too?

(d) Dogs and other animals can s __ __ __ tears.

(e) The t __ __ __ __ of dogs are used to m __ __ __ __ __ __ their eyes.

Word Tip			
▮ human	▮ often	▮ laugh	▮ cry
▮ sad	▮ other	▮ 눈물을 흘리다	▮ 사용되다
▮ 촉촉하게 하다	▮ 표현하다	▮ 행복	▮ 또한, 역시

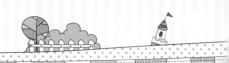

Vocabulary I

Let's complete the crossword puzzle.

Words

HUMAN (▼) / LAUGH (▶) / ANIMAL (▶)

SMILE (▶) / CRY (▶) / TEAR (▼)

Vocabulary Ⅱ

Write down the matching words.

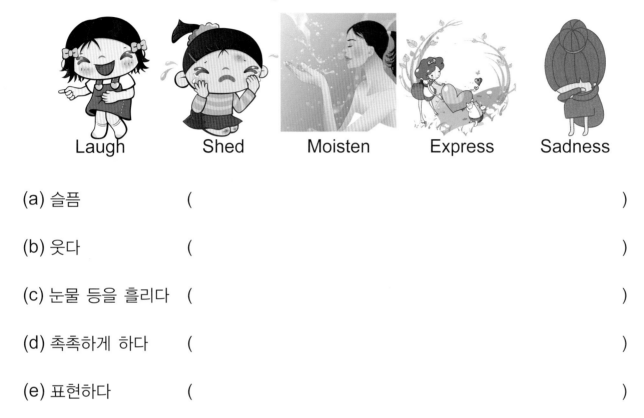

| Laugh | Shed | Moisten | Express | Sadness |

(a) 슬픔   (   )

(b) 웃다   (   )

(c) 눈물 등을 흘리다   (   )

(d) 촉촉하게 하다   (   )

(e) 표현하다   (   )

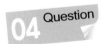
Comprehension

Look at the sentences below. Decide if they are true or false!

(a) Dogs cry to express sadness.   O / X

(b) Dogs cannot shed tears.   O / X

(c) Only humans can smile to express happiness.   O / X

(d) Humans cry when they are sad.   O / X

How Many Eyes Do Spiders Have?

Spiders are interesting animals. There are more than 38,000 kinds of spiders in the world. Spiders have eight legs. Their legs are very long. Then, how many eyes do they have? Most animals on Earth have two eyes. But most spiders have eight eyes! Some spiders have only six eyes. If you see a spider, try to count its eyes!

Staff reporter Daniel Chang

Let's look at the picture. Fill in the blanks and complete the sentences.

① long   ② animals   ③ Earth   ④ eyes   ⑤ legs

(a) Spiders are interesting (   ).

(b) Spiders have eight (   ).

(c) The legs of spiders are very (   ).

(d) Most animals on (   ) have two eyes.

(e) Most spiders have eight (   ).

Word Tip			
▮ interesting	▮ kind	▮ leg	▮ long
_____	_____	_____	_____
▮ most	▮ 지구	▮ 몇몇의	▮ 세다
_____	_____	_____	_____

 **Grammar**

Circle the right answers.

(a) There are [**more** / less / most] than 38,000 kinds of spiders in the world.

(b) If you see a spider, try [**count** / to count / counted] its eyes.

(c) How [**much** / long / many] eyes do spiders have?

(d) Did you know that some spiders [**have** / has / are] only six eyes?

(e) Have you ever [**saw** / seen / see] the eight-eyed spider?

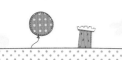

Vocabulary

Find the hidden words in the puzzle below. The words are from the article.

V	B	M	F	W	S	L	B	R	C
Y	E	A	R	A	V	I	I	N	W
U	S	W	I	S	G	S	R	C	R
O	P	G	E	H	E	T	D	S	J
K	I	N	D	E	R	E	U	R	L
P	D	Y	D	V	S	N	E	Y	E
S	E	I	K	H	H	G	I	R	I
V	R	T	D	W	F	L	Q	O	G
M	O	R	N	E	N	G	K	I	H
X	G	H	K	T	C	O	U	N	T

Words

SPIDER / KIND / EYE / EIGHT / COUNT

I'm a Very Lucky Boy!

Pearls are very beautiful and expensive. Recently, a very lucky boy in the US found a pearl while eating oysters! His name is Brice Hoza and he is 11 years old. Earlier this year, he went to a restaurant with his grandma for lunch. Brice ordered fried oysters and found a pearl inside an oyster! What a lucky boy!

Staff reporter Erica Choi

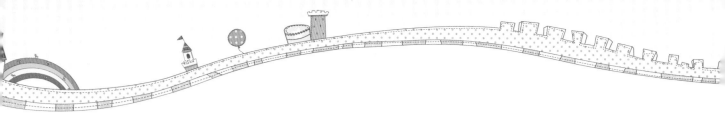

Writing I

Use the words below to make the sentences.

> lunch / expensive / pearl / oyster

(a) Who is the boy in the picture?

→ He is an 11-year-old boy who found a _____ inside an _____.

(b) How could he find a pearl?

→ He found a pearl when _____ _____.

(c) Why do you think he is lucky?

→ Because pearls are very _____.

Word Tip			
‖ pearl	‖ expensive	‖ found (find의 과거형)	‖ oyster
_____	_____	_____	_____
‖ 레스토랑, 식당	‖ 주문하다	‖ ~안에	
_____	_____	_____	

Grammar

Circle the right words to complete the sentences.

(a) Pearls are very beautiful and [**expensive** / cheap / useless].

(b) Recently, a very lucky boy in the US [**founded** / found / find] a pearl while eating oysters!

(c) Earlier this month, he [**go** / went / goes] to a restaurant with his grandma for lunch.

(d) Brice ordered fried oysters and found a pearl [**inside** / outside / under] an oyster!

Writing II

Write your own story describing the picture below.

Hint: Be creative!

What can you imagine seeing the pearl inside a shell?

_____

_____

_____

_____

_____

_____

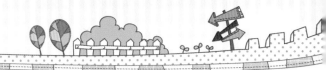

 **Question** **Vocabulary**

Let's solve the crossword puzzle below.

Across
① The opposite meaning of 'cheap'
② It means an old lady.

Down
③ A hard and round one which is found inside shells
④ It's the opposite word for 'outside'.

Can Gorillas Walk Like Humans?

Most animals walk on four legs. But can gorillas walk upright like humans? Normally, they get around on all four legs. But if you visit a zoo in Kent, England, you can see a walking gorilla! His name is Ambam and he is 21 years old. He became famous with his unusual habit of walking upright! Many people visit the zoo to see the special gorilla.

Staff reporter Daniel Chang

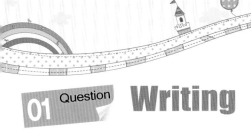

Writing

Let's look at the picture. Fill in the blanks and complete the sentences.

① like   ② four   ③ gorilla   ④ walking   ⑤ back

(a) You can see a (   ) in the picture.

(b) The gorilla is looking (   ).

(c) Can gorillas walk (   ) humans?

(d) Gorillas get around on all (   ) legs.

(e) If you visit a zoo in Kent, England, you can see a (   ) gorilla.

Word Tip

most	walk on four legs	walk upright	normally
_____	_____	_____	_____
get around	방문하다	걸어 다니는	~로 유명해지다
_____	_____	_____	_____
특이한, 흔치 않은	습관	특별한	
_____	_____	_____	

 **Grammar**

Circle the right answers.

(a) The gorilla's name is Ambam and he is 21 [**year** / years / ages] old.

(b) Ambam became famous with his unusual habit of [**walk** / walked / walking] upright.

(c) Many people [**visit** / visited / will visit] the zoo to see the special gorilla every day.

(d) What kinds of animals [**was** / do / does] you like?

(e) [**More** / Most / Every] animals walk on four legs.

 **Vocabulary**

Find the hidden words in the puzzle below. The words are from the article.

L	E	G	T	U	L	L	L	R	L
Y	I	O	R	A	M	I	T	N	W
U	G	R	I	S	O	S	U	C	R
O	H	I	U	R	E	T	D	S	J
K	T	L	D	E	R	E	K	R	L
P	D	L	D	V	S	S	S	Y	V
S	N	A	M	E	O	T	T	O	I
V	R	T	D	W	F	U	Y	A	S
M	O	R	N	E	N	D	E	L	I
X	G	H	K	T	H	A	B	I	T

Words

VISIT / GORILLA / LEG / NAME / HABIT

Be Careful When Enjoying Food Outside

In spring, many children go on a picnic with their family. They usually enjoy Kimbab, sandwich, or fried chicken outside. They are very delicious.

But you have to be careful when eating them. In spring, food can go bad easily. This is because the weather gets warmer. If you feel sick after eating something, tell your mom or dad right away.

Staff reporter Crystal Lim

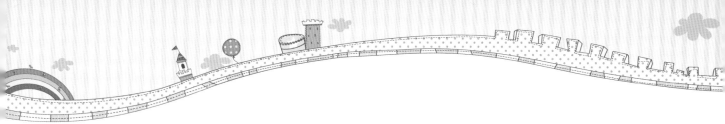

 **Writing**

Complete the sentences by filling in the blanks.

(a) In spring, many children go on a **p** __ __ __ __ __ with their family.

(b) But you have to be **c** __ __ __ __ __ __ when eating food.

(c) In spring, food can **g** __ **b** __ __ easily.

(d) This is because the weather gets **w** __ __ __ __ __ .

 **Vocabulary** I

Let's complete the crossword puzzle.

Words

PICNIC (▼) / OUTSIDE (▶)

DELICIOUS (▼) / AWAY (▼) / CAREFUL (▶)

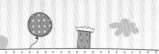

03 Question **Vocabulary II**

Let's find the matching words.

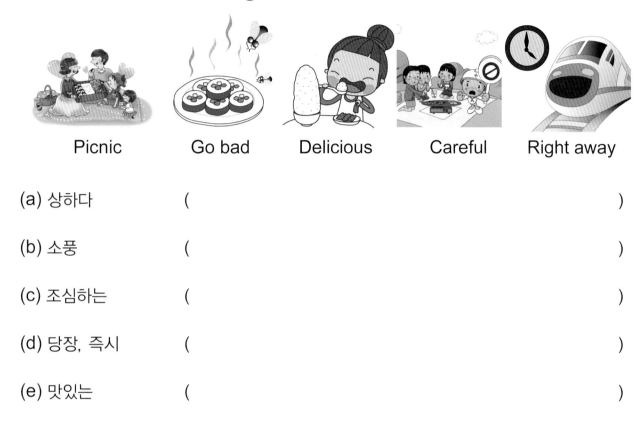

| Picnic | Go bad | Delicious | Careful | Right away |

(a) 상하다　　　　(　　　　　　　　　　　　　　)

(b) 소풍　　　　　(　　　　　　　　　　　　　　)

(c) 조심하는　　　(　　　　　　　　　　　　　　)

(d) 당장, 즉시　　(　　　　　　　　　　　　　　)

(e) 맛있는　　　　(　　　　　　　　　　　　　　)

04 Question **Comprehension**

Circle O if the statement is true, circle X if it is false.

(a) Many children go on a picnic with their family every season.　　　　O / X

(b) Children enjoy delicious food outside in spring.　　　　O / X

(c) You have to be careful when eating outside in spring.　　　　O / X

(d) Food doesn't go bad easily in spring because it is not warm enough.　　　　O / X

Drink a Lot of Water for Fresh Breath!

You have to talk to many people every day. But if you have bad breath, other people will feel uncomfortable. Don't worry. There are simple ways to keep your breath fresh. First, brush your teeth after a meal. Brushing your tongue is also important. Drinking a lot of water is helpful, too! Keeping your breath fresh is easy!

Staff reporter Crystal Lim

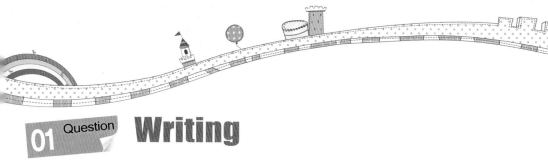

Writing

Complete the sentences by filling in the blanks.

(a) You have to **t** __ __ __ to many people every day.

(b) If you have bad breath, other people will feel **u** __ __ __ __ __ __ __ __ __ –
__ __ __ __.

(c) There are simple **w** __ __ __ to keep your breath **f** __ __ __ __.

(d) Drink a lot of **w** __ __ __ __ for fresh breath!

Word Tip			
‖ have to	‖ have bad breath	‖ uncomfortable	‖ worry
‖ simple	‖ 유지하다	‖ 상쾌한, 산뜻한	‖ 이를 닦다
‖ 식사	‖ 혀	‖ 많이	‖ 도움이 되는

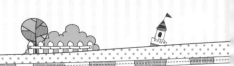

Vocabulary I

Let's complete the crossword puzzle.

Words

WORRY (▶) / SIMPLE (▼) / HELPFUL (▼)

FRESH (▶) / EASY (▼) / TEETH (▶)

03 Question **Vocabulary Ⅱ**

Let's find the matching words.

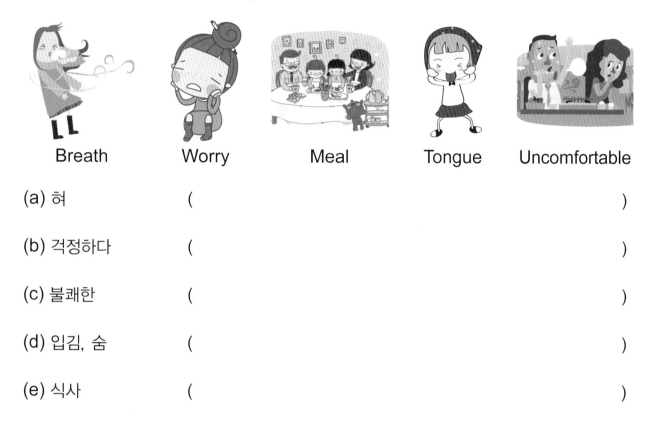

| Breath | Worry | Meal | Tongue | Uncomfortable |

(a) 혀 ( )

(b) 걱정하다 ( )

(c) 불쾌한 ( )

(d) 입김, 숨 ( )

(e) 식사 ( )

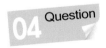

04 Question **Comprehension**

Circle O if the statement is true, circle X if it is false.

(a) You had better brush your tongue as well as your teeth.   **O / X**

(b) You have to brush your teeth once in a day.   **O / X**

(c) Drinking a lot of soda is helpful to keep your breath fresh.   **O / X**

(d) If you have bad breath, you will have difficulty making friends.   **O / X**

I Have More Than 2,000 Cats!

If you visit England, you can meet a special cat lover. Her name is Pamela Cole and she is 60 years old. Her house is full of cats! Don't worry. They are not real cats. They are ceramic cats. She spent most of her life collecting more than 2,000 ceramic cats. "I love cats very much. I will not stop collecting them!" she said. Let's see how many more cats she will collect!

Staff reporter Erica Choi

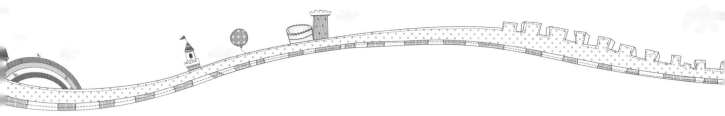

Read each question and find the right answer.

(a) What is the main topic of the article?

① An old lady who collected a lot of ceramic cats

② An old lady who collected lots of stuffed animals

③ An old lady who made a lot of ceramic cats

④ An old lady who collected a lot of ceramic dogs

(b) Write down three words that begin with 'C' in the article.

① _____

② _____

③ _____

(c) How many ceramic cats does Pamela Cole have?

She _____.

Word Tip

▮ cat lover	▮ be full of	▮ ceramic	▮ more than
_____	_____	_____	_____
▮ 모으다, 수집하다	▮ 특별한	▮ 진짜의	
_____	_____	_____	

 **Vocabulary**

Choose the right words to complete each sentence.

(a) If you _____ England, you can meet a special cat lover.

   ① visited

   ② visit

   ③ have visited

   ④ will visit

(b) Her house is _____ of cats!

   ① full

   ② nothing

   ③ without

   ④ filled

(c) She spent most of her life _____ more than 2,000 ceramic cats.

   ① collect

   ② collected

   ③ collects

   ④ collecting

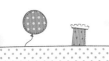

 **Comprehension II**

Look at the picture below and then answer the questions.

(a) Who is she?

① She is a grandmother who has been collecting lots of ceramic cats.

② She is a grandmother who has been making lots of ceramic cats.

③ She is a grandmother who has been selling lots of ceramic cats.

④ She is a grandmother who has been studying lots of ceramic cats.

(b) Why has she been collecting ceramic cats?

① Because she is rich.

② Because she can sell them at high price.

③ Because ceramic cats are expensive.

④ Because she loves cats.

(c) Where does she live?

① She lives in Britain.

② She lives in the United States.

③ She lives in Paris.

④ She lives in Japan.

Honey Is Good for Your Cough

Cough! Cough! It's easy to catch a cold during the freezing winter days. If you catch a cold, you will cough a lot. Coughing can give you a headache. You won't sleep well at night, either. So, what can you do when you cough a lot? Try eating a teaspoon of honey before you go to bed. It will be good for your cough and it will help you sleep well.

Staff reporter Crystal Lim

Writing

Complete the sentences by filling in the blanks.

(a) Children can **c** __ __ __ __ a **c** __ __ __ easily even in spring.

(b) **C** __ __ __ __ __ __ __ can give you a headache.

(c) You won't **s** __ __ __ __ well at night, either.

(d) Try eating a teaspoon of **h** __ __ __ __ before you go to bed.

Word Tip			
‖ cough	‖ catch a cold	‖ freezing	‖ headache
_____	_____	_____	_____
‖ not ~ either	‖ try ~ing	‖ a teaspoon of	‖ 자러 가다, 잠자리에 들다
_____	_____	_____	_____
‖ ~에 좋다			
_____			

 **Vocabulary** I

Let's complete the crossword puzzle.

Words

COUGHING (▶) / HONEY (▼) / SPRING (▼)

HELP (▶) / CHILDREN (▼)

03 Question Vocabulary II

Let's find the matching words.

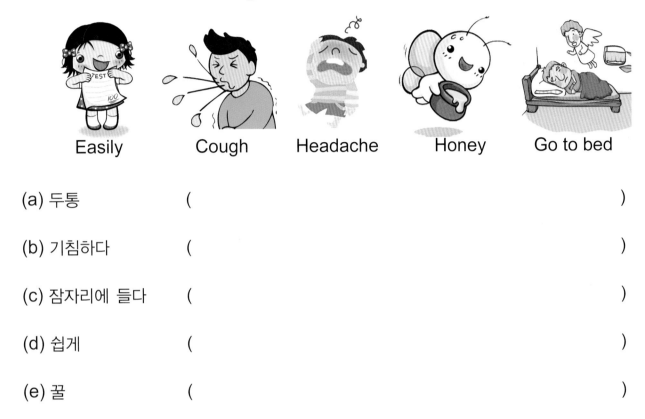

Easily   Cough   Headache   Honey   Go to bed

(a) 두통   (   )

(b) 기침하다   (   )

(c) 잠자리에 들다   (   )

(d) 쉽게   (   )

(e) 꿀   (   )

04 Question Comprehension

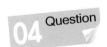

Circle O if the statement is true, circle X if it is false.

(a) Children don't catch a cold in spring because it is warm.   **O / X**

(b) You will cough a lot if you catch a cold.   **O / X**

(c) Taking a cough pill is the best way when you cough a lot.   **O / X**

(d) Eating a teaspoon of honey before you go to bed will help you not cough.   **O / X**

I Can Do Many Things without Arms and Legs!

Do you know who Ototake Hirotada is? He is a 35-year-old man from Japan. He was born without arms and legs. But he always looks happy. After graduating from Waseda University, he became a teacher. He also wrote many books. He will open a school for young children in April. "I have no arms and legs, but I can do many things!" he said with a smile. Good luck with your new school!

Staff reporter Erica Choi

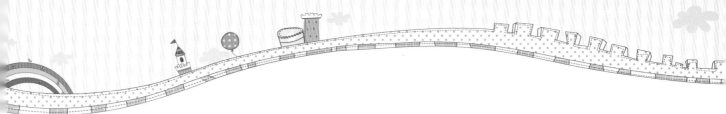

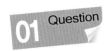

Use the words below to make the sentences.

arm / leg / happy / school

(a) Who is the man wearing a suit?

→ He is Ototake Hirotada who doesn't have _____.

(b) What made him so famous?

→ He _____ many _____ about his life.

(c) What is he planning to do in April?

→ He will open _____.

Word Tip			
▮ be born	▮ without	▮ always	▮ graduate from
_____	_____	_____	_____
▮ 웃으면서			
_____			

Grammar

Circle the right words to complete the sentences.

(a) After [**graduating** / graduate / graduated] from Waseda University, he became a teacher.

(b) He [**led** / wrote / drew] many books.

(c) He will open a school [**on** / to / for] young children in April.

(d) "I have no arms and legs, but I can [**did** / does / do] many things!"

Writing II

Write your own story describing the picture below.

Hint: Be creative!

Can you introduce him to readers?

_____

_____

_____

_____

_____

_____

_____

04 Question Vocabulary

Let's solve the crossword puzzle below.

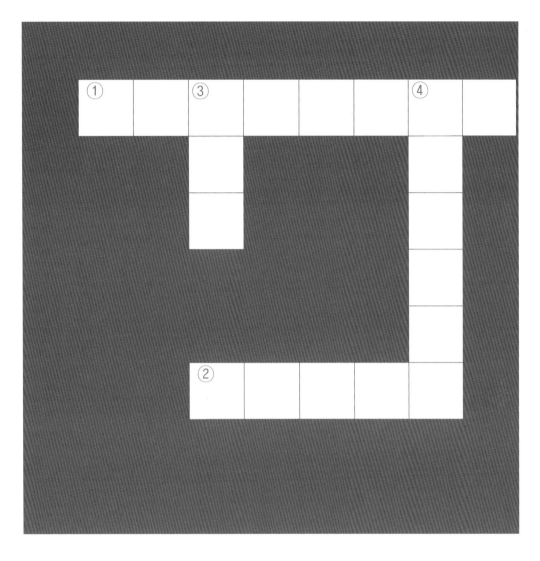

Across
① It means to complete the university successfully.
② It is similar with the word 'laugh'.

Down
③ Two long parts of your body connected with shoulders
④ A person who teaches students

What Is the Most Popular Type of Animal Milk in the World?

You may think cow milk is the world's most popular animal milk. However, more people in the world drink goat milk than any other kind! Some goats are bred specifically for milk. Goat milk is easier to digest than milk from cows. Goat milk is also used to make cheese, butter, ice cream, and even soap.

Staff reporter Daniel Chang

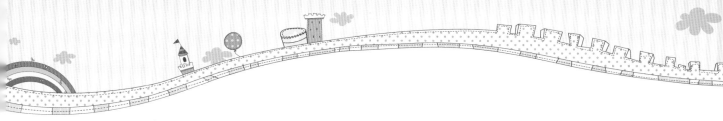

Complete the sentences by filling in the blanks.

(a) What is the most popular type of **a** __ __ __ __ __ milk in the world?

(b) More people in the world drink goat milk **t** __ __ __ any other kind.

(c) Some goats are **b** __ __ __ specifically for milk.

(d) Goat milk is easier to **d** __ __ __ __ __ than milk from cows.

(e) Goat milk is used to **m** __ __ __ cheese, ice cream, and even **s** __ __ __.

Word Tip

▮ cow	▮ popular	▮ goat	▮ kind
▮ bred	▮ specifically	▮ 더 쉬운	▮ 소화되다
▮ ~하는 데 이용되다	▮ 비누		

 **Question** # Vocabulary I

Let's complete the crossword puzzle.

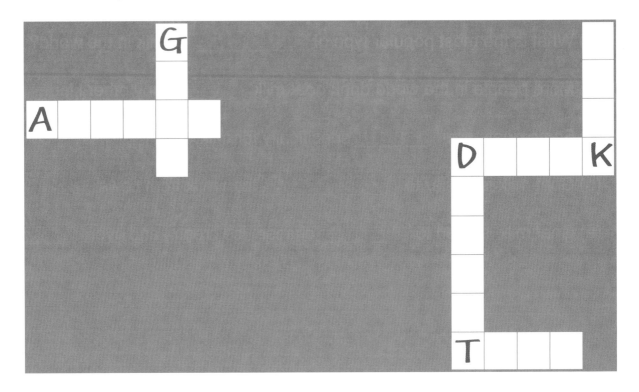

Words

GOAT (▼) / TYPE (▶) / ANIMAL (▶)

DRINK (▶) / DIGEST (▼) / MILK (▼)

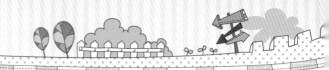

Vocabulary II

Write down the matching words.

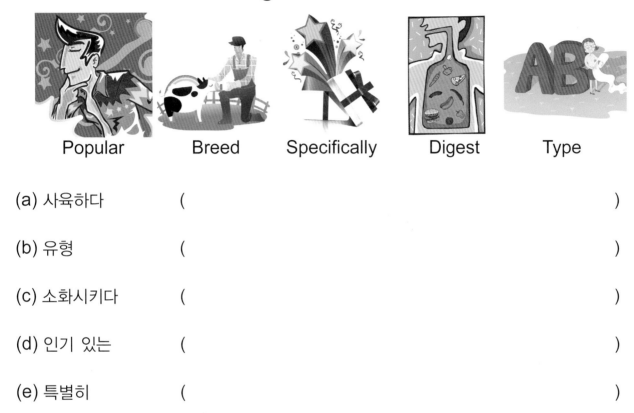

| Popular | Breed | Specifically | Digest | Type |

(a) 사육하다   (   )

(b) 유형   (   )

(c) 소화시키다   (   )

(d) 인기 있는   (   )

(e) 특별히   (   )

04 Question

Comprehension

Look at the sentences below. Decide if they are true or false!

(a) Milk is good for your body.   O / X

(b) Camel milk is the world's most popular animal milk.   O / X

(c) Cow milk is easier to digest than goat milk.   O / X

(d) Goat milk is used to make butter.   O / X

Koreans Eat Too Much Salt

Last year the Ministry of Health and Welfare said that Koreans eat too much salt. In 2009, the ministry studied about 4,000 families nationwide. It found that most Koreans eat too much salt every day. Too much salt can cause many health problems. Do not put too much salt in your food and stay healthy!

Staff reporter Daniel Chang

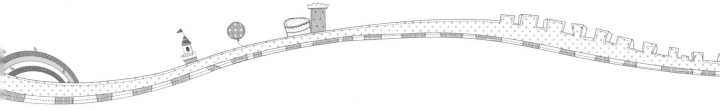

Comprehension

Let's look at the picture and fill in the blanks.

Hint: Answers are in the article.

(a) Last year the Ministry of Health and Welfare said that Koreans **e** __ __
   too much **s** __ __ __.

(b) In 2009, the ministry **s** __ __ __ __ __ __ about 4,000 families
   n __ __ __ __ __ __ __ __ __.

(c) It **f** __ __ __ __ that most Koreans eat too much salt every day.

(d) Too much salt can **c** __ __ __ __ many **h** __ __ __ __ __ problems.

Word Tip			
▌ ministry	▌ study	▌ nationwide	▌ cause
_____	_____	_____	_____
▌ 건강상 문제	▌ ~을 넣다	▌ 건강하게 지내다	
_____	_____	_____	

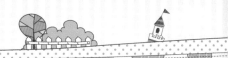

 **Vocabulary**

Connect each picture to the correct meaning.

nationwide

ⓐ

① To make something happen

cause

ⓑ

② The whole nation

stay healthy

ⓒ

③ To have a strong body and mind

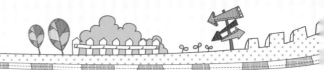

 **Writing**

Look at the picture below and write your answers.

Hint: salt, food, bad, health

(a) What is in the bottle?

→ There is _____.

(b) Where do you put salt?

→ I put salt _____.

(c) Why do you put salt in your food?

→ Because it _____.

(d) Is eating salt good for your body?

→ Eating too much _____

_____.

What Is the Smallest Planet in the Solar System?

There are eight planets in the Solar System. Later we will learn about the biggest planet. But first, what is the smallest planet? It is also the closest planet to the Sun. Yes, it's Mercury! It is also called the 'Morning Star'. This is because it shines brightly in the early morning. Why don't you get up early and find Mercury in the morning sky?

Staff reporter Samuel Sohn

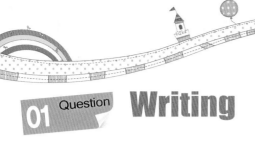

01 Question Writing

Let's look at the picture. Fill in the blanks and complete the sentences.

① called   ② smallest   ③ planet   ④ closest   ⑤ eight

(a) What is the (   ) planet in the Solar System?

(b) There are (   ) planets in the Solar System.

(c) It is the (   ) planet to the Sun.

(d) It is also (   ) the 'Morning Star'.

(e) The (   ) is Mercury.

Word Tip

▮ planet	▮ Solar System	▮ later	▮ learn
▮ the biggest	▮ the smallest	▮ 가장 가까운	▮ 수성
▮ ~라고 불리다	▮ 빛나다	▮ 밝게, 환하게	▮ ~하는 것이 어때?
▮ 일어나다			

 **Grammar**

Circle the right answers.

(a) Can you guess the name [**from** / of / at] the planet?

(b) Mercury shines brightly in the [**early** / late / short] morning.

(c) There are several planets in the Solar System – 8 planets in [whole / **total** / each] .

(d) Why don't you [make / take / **get**] up early and find Mercury in the morning sky?

(e) Have you ever [**watched** / watch / watching] the planet in the sky?

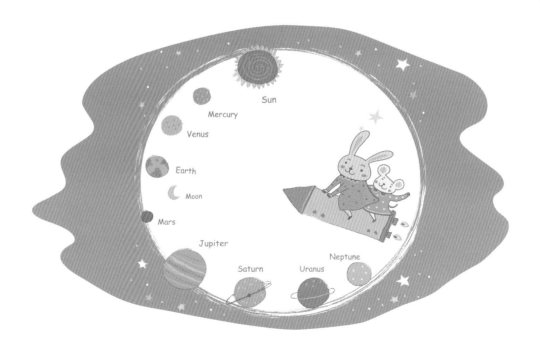

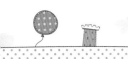 

 **Question** **Vocabulary**

Find the hidden words in the puzzle below. The words are from the article.

P	A	G	L	W	S	W	B	R	O
G	L	O	Q	A	V	H	I	N	T
W	J	A	B	S	G	G	R	C	S
L	E	G	N	H	E	M	D	S	K
H	T	I	M	E	R	C	U	R	Y
S	G	Y	G	E	T	R	F	A	N
S	H	Y	K	H	H	G	I	R	W
V	P	I	Q	W	F	L	Q	I	E
M	O	R	N	I	N	G	N	I	B
Q	E	X	P	E	N	G	I	V	E

Words
PLANET / MERCURY / SHINE / MORNING / SKY

What Is the Biggest Planet in the Solar System?

There are 8 planets in the Solar System: Mercury, Venus, Earth, Mars, Jupiter, Saturn, Uranus, and Neptune. Pluto is not a planet anymore. Do you know what the biggest planet is? It's Jupiter! It also has the most moons in the Solar System. Jupiter is mainly made of gases.

Staff reporter Samuel Sohn

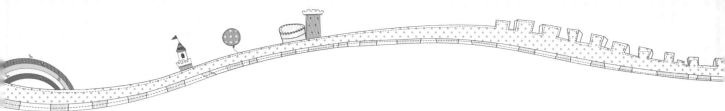

Comprehension

Which is NOT true about the article? Read the following sentences and then correct the wrong ones.

(a) There are 8 planets in the Solar System.

→ _____.

(b) Pluto is a planet.

→ _____.

(c) The smallest planet in the Solar System is Jupiter.

→ _____.

(d) Jupiter is mainly made of gases.

→ _____.

Word Tip

▍ planet	▍ Solar System	▍ Mercury	▍ Venus
_____	_____	_____	_____
▍ Earth	▍ Mars	▍ Jupiter	▍ Saturn
_____	_____	_____	_____
▍ 천왕성	▍ 해왕성	▍ 명왕성	▍ 더 이상 ~ 않다
_____	_____	_____	_____
▍ (many, much의 최상급) 가장 많은	▍ 주로	▍ ~로 만들어지다	
_____	_____	_____	

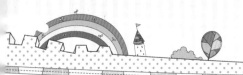

 **Grammar**

Circle the right words to complete each sentence.

(a) Have you ever [**see** / seen / seeing] the planet?

(b) Pluto is not a planet [**any** / longer / anymore] .

(c) Do you know [**what** / why / how] the biggest planet is?

(d) Jupiter has the [**more** / most / less] moons in the Solar System.

03 Question Writing

Look at the picture below. Complete the sentences to answer the questions.

(a) What is it? → It is one of _____ in Solar System.

(b) What's its name? → Its name is _____.

(c) Why is it special? → Because it is _____

in Solar System.

04 Question Vocabulary

Let's think of some words that could be used to describe Jupiter.

(a) Jupiter is the f __ __ __ __ planet in Solar System.

(b) It has an extremely s __ __ __ __ __ magnetic field.

(c) It is the third-brightest planet in the n __ __ __ __ sky.

(d) It was named a __ __ __ __ the primary Roman god, Jupiter.

ANSWERS

UNIT 01

Word Tip

여전히 / 사실 / 가장 나이 많은 /
운전자 / enjoy ~ing / excite /
often / Drive safely

1. Comprehension I
(a) ①
(b) Feel / Family / Friend
(c) started driving in 1949

2. Vocabulary
(a) ①
(b) ②
(c) ③

3. Comprehension II
(a) ①
(b) ④
(c) ②

UNIT 02

Word Tip

전 세계에 / 최고의, 꼭대기 /
생산자, 생산 국가 / 국가, 나라 / 유럽 /
그리스 / each / person / a lot of

1. Comprehension
(a) O
(b) X → People in Greece eat
the most cheese in
the world
(c) O
(d) X → Each person in
Greece eats about
28 kilograms of
cheese a year

2. Grammar
(a) Which
(b) visited
(c) eats
(d) eating

3. Writing
(a) cheese
(b) loved
(c) Greece

4. Vocabulary
(a) eating, ago
(b) rich
(c) bones
(d) popular

UNIT 03

Word Tip

사람, 인간 / 자주, 종종 / 웃다 / 울다 /
슬픈 / 다른 / shed tears /
be used / moisten / express /
happiness / either

1. Writing
(a) often
(b) laugh
(c) animals
(d) shed
(e) tears, moisten

2. Vocabulary I
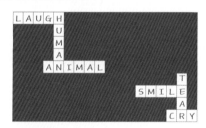

3. Vocabulary II
(a) Sadness
(b) Laugh
(c) Shed
(d) Moisten
(e) Express

4. Comprehension
(a) X
(b) X
(c) O
(d) O

UNIT 04

Word Tip

흥미로운, 재미있는 / 종류 / 다리 / 긴 /
대부분(의) / Earth / some / count

1. Writing
(a) ②
(b) ⑤
(c) ①
(d) ③
(e) ④

2. Grammar
(a) more
(b) to count
(c) many
(d) have
(e) seen

3. Vocabulary

UNIT 05

Word Tip

진주 / 비싼 / 찾았다, 발견했다 / 굴 /
restaurant / order / inside

1. Writing I
(a) pearl, oyster
(b) having lunch
(c) expensive

2. Grammar
(a) expensive
(b) found
(c) went

66

(d) inside

3. Writing II

Recently, a glittering and beautiful pearl was found inside a shell. A 98-year-old grandmother named Anny found something hard when having dinner. She was having dinner with her husband for celebrating her 98th birthday at a Chinese restaurant. "I think it's my birthday present from God! Thank you so much!" she said. What a lucky grandmother! Congratulations!

4. Vocabulary

Word Tip

대부분(의) / 네 발로 걷다 / 서서 걷다 /
보통, 정상적으로 / 돌아다니다 / visit /
walking / become famous with ~ /
unusual / habit / special

1. Writing
(a) ③
(b) ⑤
(c) ①
(d) ②
(e) ④

2. Grammar
(a) years

(b) walking
(c) visit
(d) do
(e) Most

3. Vocabulary

UNIT 17

Word Tip

소풍 가다 / 주로 / 튀긴 / 밖에 /
해야 한다 / 조심하다 / 상하다 / 쉽게 /
weather / get warmer / sick /
right away

1. Writing
(a) picnic
(b) careful
(c) go bad
(d) warmer

2. Vocabulary I

3. Vocabulary II
(a) Go bad
(b) Picnic

(c) Careful
(d) Right away
(e) Delicious

4. Comprehension
(a) X
(b) O
(c) O
(d) X

UNIT 18

Word Tip

해야 한다 / 입 냄새가 나다 / 불쾌한 /
걱정하다 / 간단한 / keep / fresh /
brush one's teeth / meal / tongue /
a lot of / helpful

1. Writing
(a) talk
(b) uncomfortable
(c) ways, fresh
(d) water

2. Vocabulary I

3. Vocabulary II
(a) Tongue
(b) Worry
(c) Uncomfortable
(d) Breath
(e) Meal

4. Comprehension
(a) O
(b) X
(c) X
(d) O

고양이 애호가 / ~로 가득 차다 / 도자기 / ~보다 많은 / collect / special / real

1. Comprehension I
(a) ①
(b) Cat / Ceramic / Collect
(c) has more than 2,000

2. Vocabulary
(a) ②
(b) ①
(c) ④

3. Comprehension II
(a) ①
(b) ④
(c) ①

Word Tip
기침하다 / 감기에 걸리다 / 매우 추운 / 두통 / ~도 아니다 / ~ 해보다 / 한 숟가락 / go to bed / be good for ~

1. Writing
(a) catch, cold
(b) Coughing
(c) sleep
(d) honey

2. Vocabulary I

3. Vocabulary II
(a) Headache
(b) Cough
(c) Go to bed
(d) Easily
(e) Honey

4. Comprehension
(a) X
(b) O
(c) X
(d) O

Word Tip
태어나다 / ~없이 / 늘, 항상 / ~을 졸업하다 / with a smile

1. Writing I
(a) arms and legs
(b) wrote, books
(c) a school for young children

2. Grammar
(a) graduating
(b) wrote
(c) for
(d) do

3. Writing II
Ototake Hirotada. It's the name of the small giant man in the picture. He was born in Japan 35 years ago. What can you notice from this picture?
Yes, he lives without arms and legs. He was born like this. Apparently, it must have been difficult to live without arms and legs. However, he always looks happy and gives courage to us.

4. Vocabulary

Word Tip
소 / 인기 있는 / 염소 / 종류 / breed(기르다)의 과거·과거분사 / 특별히 / easier / digest / be used / soap

1. Writing
(a) animal
(b) than
(c) bred
(d) digest
(e) make, soap

2. Vocabulary I

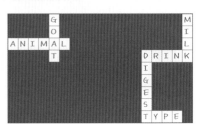

3. Vocabulary II
(a) Breed
(b) Type
(c) Digest
(d) Popular
(e) Specifically

4. Comprehension
(a) O
(b) X
(c) X
(d) O

UNIT 13

(정부) 부처 / 연구 / 전국적인 /
~을 야기하다, 초래하다 /
health problem / put / stay healthy

1. Comprehension
(a) eat, salt
(b) studied, nationwide
(c) found
(d) cause, health

2. Vocabulary
ⓐ – ②
ⓑ – ①
ⓒ – ③

3. Writing
(a) There is salt in the bottle
(b) I put salt in my French
    fries
(c) Because it is too bland for
    me
(d) Eating too much salt is no
    good. It can cause many
    health problems

UNIT 14

행성 / 태양계 / 나중에 / 배우다 /
가장 큰 / 가장 작은 / the closest /
Mercury / be called / shine /
brightly / Why don't you ~? / get up

1. Writing
(a) ②
(b) ⑤
(c) ④
(d) ①
(e) ③

2. Grammar
(a) of
(b) early
(c) total

(d) get
(e) watched

3. Vocabulary

UNIT 15

행성 / 태양계 / 수성 / 금성 / 지구 /
화성 / 목성 / 토성 / Uranus /
Neptune / Pluto /
be not ~ anymore / most /
mainly / be made of ~

1. Comprehension
(a) O
(b) X → Pluto is not a planet
(c) X → The biggest planet in
        the Solar System is
        Jupiter
(d) O

2. Grammar
(a) seen
(b) anymore
(c) what
(d) most

3. Writing
(a) planets
(b) Jupiter
(c) the biggest planet

4. Vocabulary
(a) fifth
(b) strong

(c) night
(d) after